CONTINUUM

ALSO BY NINA CASSIAN

Ambit (Ambitus), 1969

Time Devouring: Selected Poems (Cronofagie), 1969

Requiem (Recviem), 1971

The Big Conjugation (Marea conjugare), 1971

Lotto Poems (Loto poeme), 1972

Suave (Suave), 1974

Spectacle in the Open-Air: Selected Love Poems (Spectacol in aer liber), 1974

One hundred poems (O sută de poeme), 1974

Orbits (Viraje), 1978

For Mercy (Indurare), 1981

Count Down (Numărătoarea inversa), 1983

Fighting Chaos (Cearta cu haosul), 1993

The Unmaking of the World (Desfacere lumii), 1997

The Avantgarde Never Dies, Never Surrenders (Avangarda nu moare, şi nu se predă), 2007

FICTION IN ROMANIAN

You're Terrific—I'm Leaving You: (Atît de grozavă şi adio), 1971

Fictitious Confessions (Confidenţe fictive), 1974

Vacation Games (Jocuri de vacanţă), 1984

TRANSLATIONS

Shakespeare (*The Tempest, A Midsummer Night's Dream, Hamlet*),
Morgenstern, Brecht, Celan, Ritsos, Mayakovsky, Chukovsky,
and others

TINUUM CONTINUUM CO

Poems

Nina Cassian

W. W. Norton & Company
New York   London

Copyright © 2008 by Nina Cassian
First American Edition 2009

For information about permission to reproduce selections from this
book, write to Permissions, W. W. Norton & Company, Inc.,
500 Fifth Avenue, New York, NY 10110

For information about special discounts for bulk purchases, please
contact W. W. Norton Special Sales at specialsales@wwnorton.com or
800-233-4830

Manufacturing by Courier Westford
Book design by Dana Sloan
Production manager: Julia Druskin

Library of Congress Cataloging-in-Publication Data

Cassian, Nina.
  Continuum : poems / Nina Cassian.—1st American ed.
     p. cm.
  Collection spanning nearly sixty years including both new English
compositions and translations by the author of her work in Romanian.
  ISBN 978-0-393-06766-8
  I. Title.
  PC840.13.A9C66 2009
  859'.134—dc22

                                                                    2008047766

W. W. Norton & Company, Inc.
500 Fifth Avenue, New York, N.Y. 10110
www.wwnorton.com

W. W. Norton & Company Ltd.
Castle House, 75/76 Wells Street, London W1T 3QT

1 2 3 4 5 6 7 8 9 0

To Maurice Edwards,

my husband,

who almost forced this book out of me,

helping my essential survival

CONTENTS

ACKNOWLEDGMENTS

The poem "My Last Book" was included in the anthology *Answering Back,* edited by Carol Ann Duffy (Picador, 2007). Four poems first appeared in a somewhat different form in the chapbook *Something Old, Something New* (Fameorshame Press, 2002): "It Wasn't Meant to Happen," "At Sylvia's Grave," "Territorial Imperative" (now called "Intolerant Landscape"), and "On a Beckett Theme."

"Letters" is a considerably revised version from the one that appeared in two earlier collections.

AUTHOR'S NOTE

This book contains recent poems (as of 2007) and older ones (starting in 1947), some written directly in English, others transposed in English from the Romanian original—by the author.

Continuum doesn't imply a stylistic continuity, but rather a creative urge spanning six decades—with no vacations and no retirement.

REMEMBER

Child Descending a Slope on a Scooter

Speeding down a slope when a child,
you feel immortal—like motion itself.
Air wraps around your face
like a colored, diaphanous veil,
and you interweave with the trees
as if passing through a dense, green torrent
flowing in the opposite direction.

You're not afraid—even when you encounter
ovoid houses, deformed by speed,
you slide along, beside them, among them,
vertiginously, on the smooth asphalt
woven in parallel threads.
You glide through the streets' assembly line
in perpetual motion,
you feel no muscular effort,
you're only worried about that point
where by all means you'll have to stop
because of that dog, slumbering in the middle of the road,
or a catapulting cascade of birds,
or a child, another child,
running headlong into you from the opposite direction,
from another assembly line,
propelled by a similar motion,
vertiginously.
All you have to do
is not stop,
go through him, or let him go through you,
borrowing for a second the contour of his body,

acquiring for a second the nuance of his eyes,
and, then, keep on running,
with the wind's veil over your face,
until the street winds up
in a plain flat surface
on which you might, eventually, lie down
finally, finally,
and let yourself be swept away
by the earth's rotation . . .

Origins

River, I have known your source:
    sparkling water crotcheting quickly through
    rock's rigid garment. Yes, I knew,
river. I have known your source.

With my palm I touched your coolness
    and beyond, a splendor not to miss,
    the new grass was waiting for your kiss.
With my palm I touched your coolness.

Black and red was rock's eternal shape
    sculpted by the wind, from head to bottom,
    in harsh summers, winters, long forgotten.
Black and red was rock's eternal shape.

And so, I would never leave the source.
    Bathed and christened in, and bright
    in its primordial, holy light,
No, no, I would never leave the source.

My Father

My father now fills the world
with his being. I presume
he grew immensely in approaching
the supreme hour, DOOM . . .

His baldness is the moon itself
as he steps from shore to shore.
He was never so saintly
and he's more earthly than ever before.

My father abandons my flesh.
I keep his eyeglasses instead,
to wear them when the dream comes by,
not to be blinded or fall out of bed.

I Have to Sleep

No matter what happens,
I have to sleep.
Somebody's dying—
I have to sleep.
I won't share my portion
of sleep with anyone
because, dear sirs,
when I sleep,
I dream of my late lover
and my deceased father
and I treat them nicely,
much more so in my sleep
than I did when awake.
Besides, in sleep, my dead cells
turn into clean, pure gold,
so that I can revive at dawn anew,
so that I can wander, dear readers, among you.

Vacation

The sea ejected two blue bodies.
Stars could have shone from them.
It was said the bodies were ours,
and good Samaritans were trying to rinse us.

The blue color was hard to remove.
Then night came—the color murderer.
The new moon was in a hurry
to spill its drink before dawn gulped it.

Finally, discolored, we woke up, we made love.
The sea rose out of its vest—the orange monocle.
It was time for us to be like everybody else.

We boiled noble fish in a pot,
and in the city with almost no trees, but a lot of neon,
we dressed conventionally and put our eyeglasses on.

Summer X-Rays

Fabulous days
with endless swims,
with algae around my waist
and convex tears on my cheeks.

Far away on the shore:
children shouting,
dogs with golden rings
circling their muzzles,
and rumors of abandoned memories.

I know what's awaiting me—
the winter of my discontent.
I have a reservation
outside on a hard bench
holding a bag of frostbitten potatoes.

That's why I swim so far out,
willing prisoner
inside the sea's immense green magnifying glass.

II.

Despite all my inner crumblings,
I'm still able to recognize a perfect day:
sea without shadow,
sky without wrinkles,
air hovering over me like a blessing.

How did this day escape
the aggressor's edicts?
I'm not entitled to it,
my well-being is not permitted.

Drunk, as with some hint of freedom,
we bump into each other,
and we laugh raucously
on an acutely superstitious scale
knowing that it's forbidden.

Could it be just a trap
this perfection
this impeccable air,
this water unpolluted by fear?

Let's savor it as long as we can:
quickly, quickly, quickly.

Moon

I saw you, moon,
the very same,
rising from the sea
like the red snout of a leech
made of shadow and water,
kissing and sucking my forehead bone,
then abandoning my body
to climb into the black and empty sky—

I saw you,
with traces of human steps on your face,
yet still the same in the eternity
of the distance between us,
me, drained of blood, only by looking at you,
and remaining pale a long time
after your disappearance.

All the events that took place
between you and me,
in the shape of a key, of a dog, of a letter,
they all mix when you rise from the sea,
they mingle and sound, for a moment,
with the sound of a key, of a dog, of a letter,
until the sand shivers and shudders
and cold hands emerge
from the water's surface.

You, the same, poisonous, greedy
you, who kills by indifference,

murderous neighbor,
disguised like a fruit or a woman
with a mask of kindness and sleep,
and young, young
like barrenness itself . . .

Utopia Unlimited

These tools were good, at first,
to cut, to slash, to stab—but then
they seemed too petty, too inefficient.

So other tools were soon invented,
which could wipe out a man
as easily as you wipe off a stain,
making him vanish—nobody would care—
in the transparent coffins of the air.

These tools were called weapons of mass destruction.
And if iron was not used to make a plow,
and if steel did not give birth to bridges,
it is because they were hungry for death.

But this was long ago and far away,
when there was always war on earth.
Indeed, it's hard for us to understand—
for us who live, for centuries, in peace . . .

But blood, a stubborn witness, takes the stand.

Mother

I. VIGIL

I grew beautiful as mother was dying.
I wept and kept vigil. And the tears
made my face look young and shiny, like a mirror.

The toughest criminal could have entered and split
my head in two—and she would not have raised her hand in
    my defense.

And yet I was beautiful, the way she always wanted me to be,
and spring came: damp, green
vegetal stumps menacing the garden,
scratching it until it bled.

But so far mother was dying,
ignoring everything and everyone.

Still I was beautiful as I stood counting
her fighting breaths, her fierce struggle,
but she did not see me.

And no one is going to see me like that—
ever, from now on.

II. THE BRIDE

They carried her like a bride,
in white lace,

and our poor, beautiful house
was left like a ship without sails,
and all three
of my fates
were very much embarrassed.
They predicted good and evil
but never mentioned death to me.

How could they face me now?
How could they tell me
that something happened which shouldn't have happened,
announcing a common destiny
to all people and all things?
That's what they tell themselves
and blame themselves for. That's what they mostly hate,
my poor three fates.

III. CENOTAPH

The winter was coming to an end. Now it begins.
I still remain on top of you and feel to the core
how your silver nails grow cold.
No one should ever question me anymore.

How beautiful your forehead, you, lying flat,
ingested now by the Horizontal.
You, my transparent, gala dead one.
In the perpetual March-to-November

confusion of the seasons. You
are the link which bridges all together,
upon which I come swimming back to you.

Just Like That

Just like that, just like that, twisting, shrinking, flinching,
distorted like a length of yarn on fire—
that's how I'm supposed to climb the so-called steps to
    perfection,
while others wander like angels, waltzing,
holding on one shoulder a box of cookies,
and on the other, a barbell,
moon on one end, sun on the other.

Night of Revelations

Where is my lovely smile now,
that foolish and divine smile of mine,
emanating like an aroma from my features,
so much so that it might have generated
a sect of smilers whose deity I would become?

Indeed, it fascinated the weak spirited
by an immobility so solar
that it seemed to be the movement
—both static and vertiginous—
of Fate itself.

Mine was the smile of the golden idol
for whom wrath, forgiveness, love, indifference
bore the same expression
like a universal scent of matter.

One night I realized
that I wasn't smiling anymore.
My face was void,
and a terrible absence weighed on it.

The world was pressing down on my face without letup.
My smile no longer opposed it.
I made weird gestures. Someone looking at me
would have thought I was wrestling the Invisible Man.

And as it weighed on my face, the world
dug into the middle of my forehead,

on just that spot where, it is said,
the Third Eye should appear.

And yes, at dawn, there it was—
the eye all by itself, shining alone,
the eye standing eye-to-eye with itself
—an eye for an eye,—
the eye in the bird's-eye view,
the eye from every point of view.

CREATURES
FROM
INNER SPACE

Poets

Those fifth-wheel fanatics,
those dangerous lunar horsemen,
their green hair obstructing their eyes
so they can't see where they're heading,
hands disconnected from reins,
bodies estranged from horses
and saddles.
Just elongated nudes
under the folds of night
which they rip in their galloping,
just blind nudes riding up to that globe where an Enormous
    Finger
once drew a mouth and three nostrils
and hung a tear of dust
onto a nonexistent eye,
and wrote something remote
—something that no one can decode.

Not a Raven

A bird—very close to me,
a kind of relative,
showed me a hidden spring
in the woods.
I tasted it,
and suddenly leaves covered my body.
Two squirrels
jumped on my shoulders.
The spring itself
engulfed my legs
like a transparent weed.

We stayed like this
till evening fell.

Then the bird announced to me
my youth had come to an end.

A Night Event

The sea smelled of grapes
when I walked through the yard that night.

But my dog, leashed to his kennel,
was suddenly scared of me.

He twisted his short rope, yelping horribly, though
I didn't do anything but call out his name tenderly.

He pulled more violently on the rope, then stretched out
flat on the ground, waiting for me to kill him.

What happened? I must have looked very tall
or hunchbacked or very ghostly—I don't know.

But ever since, I've been frightened by my own aspect
and its paradoxical effect.

Malignant Feast

The trivial noises of the petty tyrants
to whom power means
    to slurp and burp at official dinners,
and whose favorite dish is made up of
        violinists,
           including their violins.

A Metaphor

Let's not allow our weaknesses
—like some hungry, insinuating cats—
to chase our pots and pans,
to shed hair on our bedsheets,
to insult our hearing
with their heartbreaking, hypocritical
meowing.

If you pity them for an instant,
and scratch their bony heads,
they won't ever leave.
They'll take on perfect shapes,
like long-molded amphorae,
and become decorative and indispensable.

Leave them at the door,
those vagabonds of old slums.
Don't allow their sinuous tails
to encircle the furniture's ankles
or ours.

"Oh, but I love cats—
as I love my weaknesses."

Two Fables

Your head is so much like an ostrich egg,
while I wear my baby-poem in the front pocket of my apron
like a kangaroo.

Are we naked like them?
Only when we wear emperors' clothes.

God's inventiveness
confuses our Cartesianism.

Look at elephants
with their hanging skin of very old men . . .

Look at birds,
those creatures without ears . . .

The zoo is illogical.

Orangutan

He stretched out his arm, he opened his palm,
staring at us
like a beggar,
like an actor showing off:
"Did you like my performance?"—
or was he just inviting us
to join him on his branch?

For long minutes
we watched his gestures,
wondering who was watching whom . . .

Should we have joined him on his branch
in our relentless search for ancestors?
or ultimately addressed him,
"Lord Hamlet!"—
since the only thing missing in his open hand
was Yorick's skull.

Sketch

The beach whisks its moustaches
of dry weeds.
The wind blows
over those cheerful solitudes.
The orange-colored dog
squats under the big tent
and contemplates the sea.
What's his name? I don't know.
Maybe Kronos, maybe Hades.
What a funny show,
gentlemen and ladies!

I hide in the sand,
I hide in the fog.
The wind shouldn't touch me.
Nor should the dog.

Scared

The tiny hare, caught by hand
in a field full of brambles,
was, I believe, not even a month old.
One of his ears trembled a bit,
and, alone with his primal fear,
he looked about wildly and strangely.

Deaf to all voices and lures,
he spread so much fear
that we didn't dare
to touch his little gray head,
for we couldn't stand
the fear which emanated from him.

He didn't have time to overcome the scare.
At night the cat surreptiously devoured the hare.

Tyrants

I knew only a few of them personally.
Between me and them
—like a protective deity—
stood my colossal ignorance,
a bodacious woman of stone,
related to the Statue of Liberty,
my dignity,
part of the Infinite Column.

It happened, nevertheless,
in a moment of recklessness,
I was touched by one or the other
of those tyrants.
Their glare dug
invisible craters into my flesh,
They shoved me about
with their padded shoulders.

They are responsible
for all the tombs
archeologists discover in me.

However remotely I stood from them,
my destiny seemed to be that of an obedient dog
listening with ears pricked up
to their commands.

Seemingly . . .

In a Submarine

They come close to the window,
blue-eyed, yellow-tailed,
others, black-and-white-striped,
gray and purple,
among moving forests,
among mysterious constructions—
I wonder who lives in the slums
and who in the palaces
(why should class concerns always follow me?)
amidst multicolored particles snowing,
veils floating and ribbons flying,
as in a ballroom on New Year's Eve.

Here's a shark,
there's a tortoise—
the aggressive and the passive one
(why do I always acknowledge conflicts?)

I am alone and human
in a soundless universe—
though my submarine is not yellow.
I need a song!

Aquarium

One day I saw a shark in an aquarium,
a small shark, an offspring of a shark,
a tiny shark so bald and svelte and slim—
in his eyes, crime was already starting to blink,
and was destined to grow along with him.

Thrashing about, he slammed between the four glass walls
with a cold restlessness, aiming to shatter them;
his teeth, sparkling like a cynical frost
crooked in the alveola of his curved mouth.

Each time his long muscled body
popped up greedily, I felt horror,
as in a dream one tries in vain to dissipate.
Cruelty was watching me through the window.
And it came and went and had a pink mouth,
hidden down toward its belly, open in hate.

Once in an aquarium, like in a hypnosis,
I watched a baby shark swimming.

Framed

They always deny me something:
an orange, a poem, my human status—
my identity, more and more uncertain;
in vain I sign my name to all these books,
my name—a convention,
my being—an abstraction,
distinguishing marks—none.
(. . . Oh yes: an eruption of pride on my left cheek.)
Finally, the denials which besiege me
shape my existence
like the throwing of knives at the circus
that pierce the backdrop,
outline the perfect contour
of the hypothetical victim.

The Hippocampus

A hippocampus, a sea horse,
kicked up onto the shore, dried out in the sun,
then brought here by myself
to these high and wintry mountains
where even memories are small.

Still salty, his skeleton,
greenish, thorny, with a missing eye,
maybe he deserves to be put
into a hilarious apocalypse.
. . . Some time ago he wore a supple coat
of waves in the Secretive Sea . . .

The exuberance of this past summer
freezes between trochaic and iambic.
It is a very narrow winter outside.
In the tall evergreens, evening falls,
and it snows over the hippocampus.

Song of the Hurdy-Gurdy Man

Oh, Johnny, Johnny dear,
I love you out of fear.

> You're the hurdy-gurdy man,
> own my future when you can.

You don't need a monkey snout
to pull fortune cookies out,

> pink and purple, yellow, green,
> the most beautiful I've seen.

Everything I love or hate,
you direct it, like my Fate.

> You're a coward and you're brave.
> You have one foot in the grave

and the other one in life—
just two feet instead of five.

> Dearest dear, my Johnny, Johnny,
> You're my tonic, my histrionic!

You're a bird and you're a fish,
neither cold nor feverish,

almost crucified, I think,
are your fins and are your wings.

—Oh, Johnny, Johnny dear,
I love you out of fear.

The Giant Petrified Locust

Arenas arose in its orbits—coliseums—
with light shining on bald platforms.
There was still a certain sadness in those elongated orbits,
though all traces of massacre were already carefully erased.

Bread and games were offered people
in the underground arenas on its half-opened jaws.
From above, from an aircraft, you couldn't tell
whether what we saw were just tents
or the massive skeleton of a slaughtered animal.

Curtains of water were hung on its shoulders
and diamond levees attached like brooches on togas;
also, seasons were created and giant trees planted,
strong and generous—vertical, frosted candelabras.

Finally, highly polished toboggan slides
were entrenched on the petrified mandible,
and liquified ingots of gold flowed through the tunnel,
covering the thin, immense, angular legs,
installing in the century and in eternity
our
new Eiffel Tower.

A New World

I had a lot of good friends,
insane like myself.
We attended gatherings,
but society intrigued against us
until we became enemies.
We bit ourselves, we poisoned each other,
we lost the idea of the immortal waltz
in time's ballroom.
The gray gent and the bald soprano
cursed away at each other.
Mr. Professor died,
asphyxiated by his own gas stove.

The intellectuals fight
head to head.
The proud one and the humble one
stutter unintelligibly.

Dear Hyperion,
what a phenomenon!

Only by Listening

Only by listening,
I know when the moon escapes the handcuff of the eclipse
and when the minuscule knives of the locust start working the
    crops.

Only by listening,
I know if the footsteps outside
are those of a soldier, or those of a dog,
or the strange meandering rustle of Judas's rope.

Parallel Destinies

(*The Story*)
While a tree was planted,
a genius was born.
They were both
equally beautiful.
The tree owned a tree harmony.
The genius, a genius harmony.
Nature was smiling in its balance.

(*The Tree's Adventure*)
"If it wasn't for the sparrows
I would have died a long time ago.
I could have enjoyed my death peacefully
without those hundred sonorous shots
in my skin, already weakened
by practicing summer,
without that ferocious swarm
of feathers, beaks, claws, shrieks—
where is my dignity
under this unfair attack?"

(*The Genius's Adventure*)
His harmony became visible
when he reproduced himself.
A strange light, like sweat,
invaded his face
when he added an object
to nature.
It was a silk butterfly

with emerald eyes,
with rigorous stains
of vegetable oil on its wings,
which he implanted
in the tree's bark—
an artificial butterfly,
almost immortal.

(*Murderous Objects*)
In the meantime,
there were other objects
ready to be used,
especially cars and weapons.
Always,
among trees and artificial butterflies,
there were those objects,
forming tribes and societies,
interfering,
making newborns grow
sharp, threatening teeth.

(*The Innocent Tree*)
From his ignorance,
a fruit emerged,
asymmetric but perfect,
hanging on a branch
but sufficiently free
to answer, when asked,
to the laws of gravity.

(*The Genius's Defense*)
Even if time tries to devour
his legs, he grows new ones,
his portrait becomes protean,
but it's harder to fight
the objects.
With a stone
you can destroy the stone's portrait:
the statue.

(*The Attack*)
The tribes, the societies,
the armies of objects
set a time for invasion,
the pictures running out of their frames.
Around the museums,
there were dirty puddles.
As for the soldiers,
all that's left of them
is a big woolen sock,
soaked by rain,
hardened by frost,
rigid like an iron.

(*The Tree's Age*)
If he didn't die in war
and always had just one leg,
he shouldn't be blamed.
He endured his adventures,

the artificial butterfly,
the sparrows.
Everything has consequences.
Nobody is spared.

(*The Genius's Age*)
Getting older, the creator remembered
a woman, a child, a tree.
He remembered himself, swimming, running,
He remembered wars, processions,
even ideas.
Because of so many memories,
he could hardly move,
as if paralyzed by fear
under an immense chandelier.

(*The End of the Story*)
And now the artist falls from heights
like the punished angel,
burning with speed,
rubbing himself against the air
populated by arms, statues, ideas
—and here he is:
the genius, dead,
buried at the foot of the dead tree,
under the balanced smile of nature.

TRAVELING

Nature

I closed another season behind me
—the river was locking itself in armor,
the woods were lacing themselves
in thin, silvery spider webs;
winter was around the corner.

No doubt I'll continue to move from one season to another,
carrying along my body which seems to be aging decently,
(I shouldn't hate myself,
I should comb my hair with some tenderness,
and kiss from time to time my arm or my knee
to keep alive their memory . . .)

Spring is around the corner.
Shiny threads of saliva decorate the trees.
My death wish loses its energy
as I move from one season to another:
da capo al fine.

On the Acropolis

And lightnings traversed the Parthenon
and the marble became dark gray as iron . . .
It was meant to be: for me to hear
the imperative voice of Zeus thundering
over me, lonely and frightened,
on the Acropolis.

And then it snowed, yes, it snowed
with thin and sharp snowflakes
on the rigid flesh of the Caryatids.
It must have been my fault,
coming from the north, where, in my country,
at this time of the year,
the oblique journey of light is long.
Maybe, I brought from the Septentrion
to these solar coasts,
the majestic shroud of winter.
Maybe, if I leave now,
everything will be transparent again
and blue dolphins will roam the sky.

Anyway, I saw, I saw a miracle,
in the decorum of mythology,
a contemporary storm.

Greece

Of course, the Acropolis was closed.
Though I climbed with wounded legs
to the top of it.
Though I wanted to be alone,
prisoner of the air between the columns . . .

I even wanted to write a poem,
but that horrible accountant stopped by,
telling me there weren't enough lines in my sonnet!
Who was the expert?

Adapting to the Environment

Rocky Greek seashores,
houses like fish scales.
I don't pray in your churches.
I don't eat your lamb.
But then: somehow I have a friend,
a white goat
with whom, three times a day,
I discuss grass, I ruminate poetry;
and then somehow I have another friend,
a gentle donkey
who carries
on his back
my tombstone
and my sins.

In an Olde English Inne

I'm cold,
useless,
sometimes drunk,
wasting my working vacation
near a fireplace, its coals burned out,
and a black cat—
talking to myself
and sometimes to the cat.

This realm is possessed by sundry ghosts,
some bearded, some feathered,
some just naked
like long, transparent fingers
playing an invisible score.

Cold, useless, drunk
and talking to myself
—while the cat's only activity
is purring.

Intolerant Landscape

Weeds, long, thin and curled,
black and yellow—dried hair
of blondes and brunettes, buried
long ago in this intolerant landscape.
(Had there been a witch hunt?)

Here I am,
near the carcass of a mill off duty
—the right spot for wasteland dirges.
A touch of rust in the woods.
(Leftovers of a murder?)

November.
How ugly this penultimate month of the year—
—the month I was born.
What remains of the sun
doesn't gild my destiny.

True, I'm here at Lumb Bank, England.
Yesteryear I was in Romania.
Surrounded by witch hunts and murders.

A Lonely Tourist

Here it is—the wild Irish Sea.
Seagulls, with their strong wings stretched out
as if crucified by the wind.
I also see a cluster of yellow flowers
similar to those in my lost garden . . .
. . . because, you see, it is spring,
and all of this happens to me, my love,
without you, here on the moors:
the miracle of breathing, the watching,
the bluish mother-of-pearl nails of water
scratching the beach.

And the sea, of course, ends in swamp.

An Unnatural Moment of Perfect Peace

Very soon, the fireworks will explode,
filling the dark sky
with enormous chrysanthemums,
with gold and platinum exclamation marks
—but so far
it's a moment of perfect tranquility,
nobody around,
the most "silent night" of
every imaginary Christmas
—by the way, the month is March,
and some imprudent apricot trees
have already given premature birth
to small, wry, wrinkled fruit.

It's an unnatural empty night
I contemplate from my solitary balcony at 9:00 p.m.

Not a soul.
Not a late homecomer.
No cars.
No wagons.
No cowboys.

Although it's Disney World,
no big-eared Mickey
nibbles on my left knee.

It's unnatural
in a world torn apart by irreconcilable conflicts
this moment of perfect peace.

I think I'm inside a glass.
Very fragile.—Hush, hush . . .

Today the Sun Is Bandaged

Today, the sun is bandaged.
Wrapped in clouds of gauze,
it doesn't bleed anymore.

Yesterday, light's hemorrhage overwhelmed everybody.
There were plenty of casualties in the camp.
People refused to wash themselves
and wandered around, smeared with blood,
proud warriors exhibiting their wounds.

Today, they're clean and healed.
Shadows that protect the camp,
wrap sadness in the willows,
bring loneliness to couples.
Pointless peace is installed.

When will we bleed again?

The South Wind

The south wind gradually cooled off the sea.
It wasn't avoiding us either, flattening
the stalks of love.
The south wind that spreads a static cold
that glooms over the water's colors without stirring them.
The south wind, the terrifying wind.

We resisted the best we could,
swimming vigorously, breaking the cold
with our kisses and the blood of our lips.
We put up orange-colored tents
which ignite at twilight like flames,
and we cried out with love
and we were the wind's most powerful foes.

Since then, when I hear
fishermen saying: the south wind is blowing . . .
—I feel like an old warrior
indebted to his wounds.

HOMAGES

O Destiny, Fate

O Destiny, Fate.
In Poe as in Satan's cauldron
I boil—and it's late.

The maiden Lenore
with her claws
writes down and draws
a curse, my identity.

Ashes on leaves,
a dim lake, Ulalume.
There is my life and my doom.
O Fate, Destiny.

Among the Great Ones

I:

To paint a winter
like Breughel,
a spring
like Botticelli,
a summer
like Van Gogh
—if my tongue were a brush
I would like to lick the seasons
whether suffocated by snow,
gracious in transparent garments
or devoured by crows.

II:

Emily, sister sublime,
you wrote with capital letters
Life and Death and Rhyme
—that's all that matters
on my island where I
learn to Live and to Die,
occasionally trying to Rhyme . . .
Does it run in the family,
Emily,
Sister Sublime?

III:

We all remember
that notorious "cloud in the pants" poet,
as he called himself—Mayakovsky.
But today let's talk
about the checkered sweater
worn by the almighty Vladimir.

That acre of wool, stripes
plowed symmetrically, right and left,
worn so tight by that titanic fellow,
hardly fits into his narrow closet
where now it's draped over a hanger;
and where, on a little table outside,
sits his death mask.

(He, who felt indebted to Japan's cherry trees
        about which he never wrote
He, who complained about wasted lightbulbs
        in broad daylight
He, who noted the llama, its daughter and its mama,
        and hated Kerensky's monstrous ears
He, who believed in the internationalism
        of the metaphor—
he would only kill himself when purity was perforated
        by the trivial bullets of Truth)

And I don't leave the room. I stay,
hoping I might postpone his death.

Poet on His Deathbed

Maybe that's the reason I came here—
to see him once more, the god of words,
to be christened by his holy tear . . .

His head, beautifully draped in death's vapor,
his hands too delicate to have been put in handcuffs
or clutching barbed wires.

Greece, why did you have to add
to your grandiose legends, though bloody,
the slow killing of Ritsos?

He filled the storage rooms of your Present
with so many provisions
that your Future becomes endless.

Here I am, kissing the phalanges of his fingers
and his immense forehead from which
his white hair gushes forth
with the vigor of his ideas.

That's the reason I came here,
crawling and humiliating myself
in the threefold curse of this summer:
loneliness, devastating heat,
Ritsos dying . . .

At Sylvia's Grave

She didn't want to do it.
She didn't want to do it.
She did it.
She vanished, winking nastily,
Putting her head in the darkness of the oven,
Trading "outside" for "inside,"
Folding the petals of her children into herself,
Covering the thorns.

She once kissed the crow on its voracious beak.
She once bit the crow's jaw.
But, then, Poetry was the real crow
Feeding on her bowels.

By your innocent grave, Sylvia,
I see a perishable November flower.

You—everlasting.

On a Beckett Theme

My eyes are missing,
my hands, my legs.
All my cells—dead ends.
My thought—wrinkled.
My knees—abstract.
My philosophy—bald.

I am reduced to essence
by a minimalist composer:
nothing happens between the tonic and the dominant.
A stubborn stereotypy
insists on do-sol, do-sol
and re-la, re-la.

I retract into you,
my fundamental crawling creature,
Molloy.

Interpreting Bach

He looks out at me from assumed portraits,
his hair mantling his head like a mellow organ;
I don't even know if those cylindrical silver locks are his,
because, look, nobody knows where on earth
the flesh, nerves and bones of the modest organist,
the blind eyes of the most clairvoyant, are scattered—
and when we tread German soil, perhaps underfoot, is Bach,
    himself,
and, of course, he's everywhere man stands upright and walks.

I focus my attention on the surface of contrary movement,
on living scales traversed back and forth by thinking,
because between two sounds there is a fundamental alliance
like that between two molecules of uranium,
like that between the two last vowels of the rigorous word
    "idea";
between two sounds there is a body-to-body tension of
    contraries,
point counterpoint,
a restless fulgurant to- and fro-ing of voices reaching a final
    concordance,
like a declaration of the rights of man,
the right to enjoy with lucidity, to suffer with lucidity,
to make of rapture and pain, steps of knowledge.

My hands meet on the surface of contrary movements,
they face each other and separate, with the concentrated
    attention

of surgical instruments cautiously exploring a human
    brain;
until, on the cold ivory keys, like icicles, a German winter
    appears,
filter of all seasons,
houses with white surfaces decorated with brown wooden slats,
like addition and multiplication symbols,
a whole familiar arithmetic,
and drain pipes from whose mouths hang long syllables of
    ice,
and ogives of frost, and the Gothic spire
with its crowing lead weathercock.

Disciplined winter!
                and in one house,
21 children with their hair caught in ponytails,
improvising mornings at the harmonium,
21 children learning how to subject their smiles, restlessness,
    astonishment
to the strict laws of the fugue—
and guiding them, a tutelary spirit, Bach himself,
with his heavy features and tubular wig,
Bach the father, the
householder.
                And so, through the aroma of snow
and the intimate vapor of coffee with milk,
I foresee an immense family orchestra, a million children
    singing

with voices fresh as snow in a pacified world,
a huge chorus of children presiding over a future announcing
    with certitude,
the beauty and purity of the earth.

And so, I envisioned an organized musical winter,
clearing the troubled soul of the German forest,
and a house in which glory is domesticated
without losing its power and magic,
a home where all the clocks move impeccably
to the invisible command of time,
and where the genius sits at the table,
breaks the bread into twelve pieces
and shares it with humanity.
Twelve sounds
wakened from their tiny cribs of ivory,
twelve sounds pointing to the truth,
like the twelve strokes announcing noon and midnight;
twelve sounds pounding like hammers and trowels on a
    flawless structure,
on a minute edifice with different states of mind,
one floor of quietude over one of torment,
and above that one of certitude,
because the father took care of his sons, his descendants
    foreordained through centuries,
the numberless heirs of numberless fortunes:

                                    twelve sounds.

And so, sentences once engraved in copper
with the precise lines of Dürer and the mysterious penumbra
    of Rembrandt,
evolve today naturally into the platinum of eternity,
because each of them is a sentence against dark inquisitions,
    perverse tortures,
against the procession of somber masks and tailed vermin,
a *lâus rationis* of grandiose and supple rigor,—
and then the father cries,
and in the calm sarabandes the sound is wrapped in mordents
    and gruppettos,
isolated like a tear in a coat of frost,
like a diamond in an exquisite setting,
it's because so many of his children died,
because, in the Passion, his son was crucified,
his terrestial son who sits at supper among his companions,
who knows the red taste of wine
("Drink ye all of it"),
the tenderness and strength of the woman,
the devotion of the friend
("If I must even die with Thee, yet will I not deny Thee"),
the cruelty of the mercenaries when they carry out their job
("and they spat on him and took the reed, and smote him on
    the head"),
the man raised to respect his work and creativity,
and the heroic sense of love for his fellow man—
and therefore that total parent
belongs to those who restore dignity and the coincidence
    between truth and beauty,

the restless dialectic of the world,
to those who give palpability to numbers and organize hope,
to those who answer questions daily,
point counterpoint—

And here I want to abandon poetry
at the boiling point when it becomes music,
and penetrate
the majestic, sonorous bastion
of the great layman,

JOHANN
SEBASTIAN!

Tristia & Inferno

I refuse to climb and to descend
those paths
to make this place more familiar to me,
this place everybody talks about,
though nothing ever happens here.

I prefer to be exiled like Ovid
(whose nickname "Naso" fits my nose)
though not at a fiendish seashore, the Pontus Euxinus,
nor between hills almost bald,
with just one wart or a tuft of hair
from long-gone forests.

I prefer to be exiled like Dante
(with whom I share the profile),
but not from Eternal Rome,
rather from my vanishing childhood
in which many things happened,
but are never mentioned.

Actually, here I am, exiled
between a pregnant yesterday
and an aborted tomorrow.

LOVE'S
BOOMERANG

Lonely

Don't sleep while I write a poem
about insomnia.
My antennae are erect
so as to catch the snoring sound
of your insensitivity.

I struggle occasionally with the petty demons
that dance in my parti-colored dreams
turning them into a compact white
—death of the spectrum
or its coronation.

Spring Snow

Scrounging—a barbaric word—
through my past,
I encounter dead butterflies
and stuffed animals
and the rag of infatuation,
also a piece torn from the flag
of love for humanity.
The days embrace themselves,
choke themselves,
enter the night.

Scrounging again, I find
wool, linen, pollen—
and purity.
It's like spring snow,
a paradoxical regeneration,
a lot of untouched, white silence
and, vanished, the shape of my lover
in the sheets.

Everything starts with the letter "S"
of Snow
everything is written cleanly
in my conscience,
and everything is quiet and fresh
and there is no butchered past.

I remain pure and fresh
as at birth.

January

Kiss me, beloved, dip
your lips into mine.
Under remote stars,
your smile seems to be snowing.

The moon holds chaste lectures
in the forum.
Your arms do not want
to hold me tight, so that I don't freeze . . .

The spark sleeps inside the flint stone.
Immobile, January stays on.

Contract

He told me I'll never marry again
or else I'll be Jesus's bride.
He was right.
He was the final, definite, ultimate
husband I had.
He died,
but he kept his authority intact,
his copyright.
I owe him all my royalties.
In his name,
I sign my name.

"How Beautiful, My Queen," he said

How beautiful you are, my love.

I see your hands traversing rain's curtains,
those silvery fixtures
more supple than the prancing Firebird . . .

I see your hands searching through night's hair
for the tiny, roaming, fragile stars
whose golden rustling
disturbs the big silence . . .

How beautiful you are, my love.
I see your hands wandering over snowy slopes,
leaving two blue traces
like those left by sleighs . . .

Your hands depart with summer.
They leave fluidly,
like two cranes with open beaks,
until they vanish . . .

Drizzle

Friendly autumn drizzles,
withered old voices—
what do you have to tell me?

Do you bring news that death is near?
That the signs of nature are discolored,
that a thin, gray blood threatens me?

What do you have to tell me, you,
friendly, warning voices?

I see light
poured on the asphalt like useless oil;
and then, I see Love
going home, through the drizzle,
Love wearing its light sandals,
its blue-green scarf
left over from last summer,
Love which does not want to believe
in cold—and wanders for hours
coughing and sneezing.

I'm not ready to die yet—
as long as this heartrending, touching, affecting lass
is limping on the sidewalk.

My Lover's Back

I inscribe on my lover's back,
with a dull pencil,
these inebriated verses
—the tattoo of my senectitude,
my poem's decrepitude.

My lover's back
is covered with thousands
of minuscule craters.
Maybe a thousand ink drops
could activate their volcanic cinder.

But my used pencil
can only write obituaries:
"Grieving, inconsolable,
my eyes drop from their orbits . . ."

It Wasn't Meant to Happen

It did. It did. He came to me,
He had a knife, he cut my shirt.
I knew, I knew I would be hurt.
I was. I was.
There were some words I could select
—I told myself—to make him stop
—but no, but no.
He had no brains, no intellect
—just a "Most Wanted" on a poster.

Before he killed me
—which he did—
all I could say was "pater noster."

Letters

I

I would have written you long ago
—but, first, I wanted to break out of solitude,
that is, out of that realm where the trees,
in prayer-position, kneel inside themselves,
as rivers also flow inside themselves,
being simultaneously body and soul,
impossible to separate; I waited too
for the spider to go away,
the spider which sketched itself with a silver pencil
on my shoulder—
and here I am now, ready to tell you
that I don't love you.

II

I lean on an inclined green tin roof
under the sun; I could slide off,
but the sunbeam nails me down,
and so does the sky projecting perpendicular clouds on me,
integrating me into its order, and I am like an idol
of greenish gold, one eye bigger than the other,
and one very long ear—those who sculpted me
were asymmetrical. I sit on a sloping roof
and I remember the oblique strand of your hair
on your forehead and your entire oblique stance
toward the universe and myself,
the angle of your body indicating a mysterious cardinal point
—and I tell you: I don't love you.

III

Your silence was so compact that I could build a city on it.
Nothing actually moved, I was building in a void,
in a dazzling void of inspired lightnings.
Once, I even built a planet,
with silky mountains in the shape of sleeping birds,
with three cascades in which I planted
seven lilac fish and, somewhere, I remember,
I buried in that invented land an object
meant for us only, only ours,
which was the true meaning of the planet, its source of
    uranium.
O, your silence—or, maybe, I didn't hear well,
maybe you were singing, or laughing, or howling
and your silence was only a specific expression
of your song, your laughter, your howl.
Maybe your silence was in fact that unknown overpopulated
    planet,
and I wasn't building in a sparkling void
but just trying to cover something already existing
the way you cover a trembling malaria patient
with a blanket and another one and then a coat,
and then four pillows, until he can't be seen anymore
—but I don't love you.

IV

I write you this fourth letter
in a wooden room, at a wooden table,
wood everywhere, an awful lot of wood,
and, everywhere, inscriptions in ink,
in crayon, by the point of a knife,
names, dates, nightingales, trains,
keys (you can unlock a train with a key
and you may crush the nightingale, paralyzed on the rail
and sign your name and set down a date). I'm scared.
Beyond the wooden frame of the window
trembles the dark sleeve of night's fir tree; one night,
you were waiting for me, it was summertime.
My books were spread out on your bed.
When I came in, I saw myself already there.
Maybe I shouldn't have replaced
my body made of books, paper, wood
with my transitory body, that's what I think now
when I don't love you.

V

If you were throwing at me
the Mondays, the Tuesdays, the Wednesdays,
Monday and Tuesday and Wednesday would slip over me
and fall on the ground, soundless.
Thursday and Friday
wouldn't hurt me anymore.

They wouldn't even leave a vaccination mark on my arm,
like a minuscule Japanese umbrella.
Thursday and Friday have no power.
Saturday is limp.
Sunday—I no longer know what Sunday means
—I don't love you.

VI

I look at myself in a mirror.
I can look younger or older, as I wish.
I can resemble an animal or a plant
or even the blueprint of a flying machine.
Over all my appearances
you once flowed like volcanic lava.
No, I didn't turn to stone—
the proof lies in the events in the mirror,
the fused seasons, the mutations
and, especially, my right hand
which, once, held your eyes
so they wouldn't fall out of their orbits,
like two immense raindrops,
that same right hand
that writes now
that, look, I don't love you.

VII

I write this last letter,
leaning on a gray wall.
I remember your oblique mouth,
your embrace that was choking me,
all the luxury of that ballroom
when my errors fell in love with each other at first sight;
the way you shattered the hourglass; how suddenly
time deserted me,
and I remember
the gesture you made, sentencing me to death.
I lean on the gray wall of a courthouse,
but all I'm telling you is:
I don't love you.
And again: I don't love you.
That's all.
I don't love you.
I don't.

FINALE

Epilogue

Between the sun and me
there is a veil of quietude
which protects my eyes
from the scratch of light
which spares my being
from the blister of knowledge
which allows my self
to breathe undisturbed.

So now the war is over
and now the love is over.
How beautiful the death
well prepared in advance.

The Experience

With so much spiraling, I get dizzy.
Events swarm around my forehead
like hummingbirds; sometimes
the sun is on my right side,
sometimes on my left.
I bang my head against these two hot gongs
and wander for a while,
powdered with an essential pollen.

Then, the gold falls away, and what's left
is coolness, like a sudden baldness.

It's then I'm aware I've reached a higher level . . .

The Big Conjugation

I, who never had any appointed functions
except the function of reproduction, I never deserved of
    anyone
but you, fair Isolde, infinite daughter of my womb,
—I, who never had any worldly ambitions
except the ambition to turn the frosty letter "I"
into the ecstatic sword separating Isolde from Tristan,
—I, who never had any chances except the chance
to live smiling, when, instead of hair or memories,
insults and spit were running down my temples,
—I, who was never in power, but had the power
to exist and to embrace you, my enemy,
and to be ready at any time to die,
—I've always had the "Haves,"—having,
had, have had, had had and Have.

Collected, Selected, Neglected . . .

. . . My poems . . .
I write them, I forget them, I misplace them! They come back,
then I change them—though they can't change the world,
they change me . . . Sometimes they disagree with me.

They are my inheritance—but who are the heirs?
Who needs this improbable, almost useless fortune, no matter
     how poor people are,
while the great oppressors maintain and adore others' poverty?
Why should I collect them (some of them are really pitiful)?
Why should I select them (am I the impartial judge of their
     supposed value)?

Better neglect them, those rags of paper and words, leave them
     on their own.

We disappear in the chilly global warming
of Stepmother Earth . . .

Metamorphosis

How long is it since
deer antlers grew on my forehead
and, on my behind, a salamander's tail?

Today,
I am neutered,
or become a domestic fowl.
I submit to conventions,
I eat regularly—
and I sleep—
my beak in my feathers.

Decay

Blue-green spots
of putrefaction
on my fingers.
Nobody warned me
that we die gradually
and visibly
—in the eyes of those
who love us
and can't help.

I should have known this
from the first moment
when the "forget-me-not"
withered in my hand,
when the first
blue-green tear
flickered in my eye,
when my first history lesson
turned rancid on the page.

Promises

I wrote a promissory note
intending to pay off my debts.
However, all I had left
was my dead childhood
in its tiny coffin.

Though not a demagogue,
in my adolescence,
I promised humanity
a harmonious existence,
like a majestic chord and accord
—but I couldn't keep my word
because the rulers of this earth
are all tone deaf . . .

Now, finally, I promise myself
—since the remaining rags of my life
continue to deteriorate—
to die in style,
peacefully,
with a smile . . .

Last Curtain

The whole night, the window stood open.
The forest entered and leaned against the wall.
A squirrel started swinging on the lamp.
Snow installed itself on my arm chair.

Toward dawn came Death to verify
whether her orders had been carried out.

I was too deep asleep
to enjoy the beautiful mise-en-scène.

Inventory

I missed
    the plane,
    the train,
    the boat,
    the camel,
    the dragonfly.

If I had died in time,
I would have attended
some of the afterlife.
Now I have to content myself
with the life before.

I'm traversing an incredible series
of unfortunate events
staged by
    Vidma (Slavic)
    Striga (Latin)
    and our familiar
    Witch!

My limbs drop into the earth.
My brain bursts into my eyes.
From so many ideas
I can hardly see!

They hit me
    with sticks,
    with stones,

with fish scales,
with oyster shards,
with bare hands—

I need help
    a crutch,
    a wheelchair,
    a parachute.

I should have died in time
to avoid this inventory.

Serenity

There'll be a time, serene, a time for hymns.
I'll underline the air with just one gesture,
and I will utter stainless words.

I will say "sky" and "brook" and I'll say "sun"
and "tear" and "music" and "immunity."
There'll be a time, a time when memory
of massacres won't reach me anymore,
turning instead into a distant breeze of poetry
as sometimes blood itself exhales.

From all that once had been promiscuous,
only the sacred will remain, and I will praise
the contrasts, reconciled, forgiven and forgiving.
So I'll say "sky" and "sun" and "music"
and sky will be, and sun will be, and music
will be around me and around the world.
I'll let the vowels all regain their halo.

And it will come, that bright, sonorous time,
a time solemn and pure, a time for hymns,
and it will come, that time. Indeed, it will!

My Last Book

How do I know
that this is my last book?
My genes are adamant.
My energy is longing for exhaustion.
The words are telling me to shut up.
Yet, in total silence,
my crippled hand
ejects sometimes a pen
to inject a poem
like a shot, an intravenous,
in the missing arms of Venus.